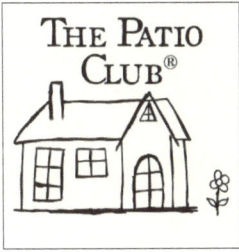

THE PATIO CLUB®

WRITTEN AND ILLUSTRATED BY

CARYN MOTTILLA

the Thanksgiving Guest

the Thanksgiving Guest

The Thanksgiving Guest
The Patio Club®
Published by Open Window Publishing
Castle Rock, CO

Publisher's Cataloging-in-Publication data

Names: Mottilla, Caryn, author.
Title: The Thanksgiving guest / by Caryn Mottilla.
Description: First trade paperback original edition. | Castle Rock [Colorado] : Open Window Publishing.
Identifiers: ISBN 978-0-9997471-0-0
Subjects: LCSH: Old age—Fiction. | Thanksgiving—Fiction. | Short stories.
BISAC: FICTION / General.
Classification: LCC PS374.O43 | DDC 813–dc22

Cover design by Caryn Mottilla

QUANTITY PURCHASES: Schools, companies, professional groups, clubs, and other organizations may qualify for special terms when ordering quantities of this title. For information, email ThePatioClub@gmail.com.

OPEN WINDOW
PUBLISHING

The Patio Club™ is dedicated to the men and women in assisted living communities, memory and Hospice care who have listened to the adventures of The Patio Club™. They expressed their hope for these stories to be published and shared with others across the country.

An Introduction to The Patio Club

The Patio Club was originally formed by two sets of sisters—Elaine and Adele from New Jersey, and Betty and Mildred from Kentucky. The women were young when they met in the 1940s. The years passed by, and later in life, the four adventurous women made a pact that after they died they would meet up and visit retirement and assisted living communities. After they passed away, they came to Happy Visions Retirement Home and liked it so much they decided to stay.

The women call themselves "The Patio Club," because they sit outside on the patio of Happy Visions. Each day, Elaine, Adele,

Betty and Mildred are surrounded by colorful sparkles, and they meet a steady stream of interesting visitors and residents who pass through Happy Visions on their way to unknown destinations.

One amazing thing is that the Patio Club can look to the sky and watch a video of each person's life. This precious gift lets the Patio Club understand the unique story that each person carries with them.

The Thanksgiving Guest

IT WAS A FEW DAYS BEFORE THANKSGIVING, AND the weather had turned colder. Dark gray clouds streaked across the late autumn sky, and squirrels ran through the crunchy brown leaves, feverishly hunting for supplies for winter.

A wooden fence with a creaky, old gate guarded the patio behind Happy Visions Retirement Home. The ground under the fence had settled more and more each year, and the fence now had plenty of room underneath it for small animals to sneak through. The squirrels took advantage

of that space, and with no trouble at all, they ran under the fence and headed to an old house that was down the street from the retirement home.

Walter the retirement home dog was often on the patio with the women of the Patio Club. Walter, however, could not go under the fence like the squirrels, because he was too big. Elaine, Adele, Betty, and Mildred laughed with delight when the squirrels made a quick getaway and Walter had to stop at the fence, obviously frustrated that he could not pursue them.

As the sparkling women watched, the squirrels ran to a house down the street, playing in the yard and searching for food. As they watched the squirrels, Elaine, Adele, Betty, and Mildred realized that since they had arrived at Happy Visions, the four women only remained on the patio and inside the small homestead. They had never felt the urge to go for a walk down the street, but just watching the squirrels made the women wonder what it would be like to leave the patio and go for a walk. Just thinking of

a new adventure brought joy to these rebellious women!

Down the street sat an old, brown house that had been built in the late 1950s. In recent years, it seemed as though the house had been deserted. In fact, the Patio Club would often see the mailman pull up to an old, rusty, black metal mailbox in front of the house and leave junk mail. Even though mail was being delivered, the women wondered who lived there, since they never saw anyone collect the mail from the mailbox.

One of the residents at Happy Visions was Edie. Every neighborhood and retirement home has someone like Edie. She always seemed to know what was going on in the retirement home and in the surrounding neighborhood.

The Patio Club decided to ask Edie if she knew who lived in the old one-story brown brick house with a lawn that looked like it had not been mowed in a very long time. An old, rusty car sat in the driveway behind the house. The car never left, and no one ever came to visit.

Although the women of the Patio Club did not know who lived in the house, they began to feel excited. They usually felt this way when they were being led to help someone new.

At lunchtime, Betty decided to approach Edie. Betty had spoken to Edie several times before and felt that Edie might be able to shed some light on who lived in the old one-story brown brick house with the rusty mailbox.

Betty found Edie sitting at a table in the dining room. Edie often sat facing the window, so she could look outside to see if anything new was happening on the street. With her bowl of soup and half-eaten sandwich in front of her, Edie was laughing as she watched the trash collectors fighting with the wind and chasing after empty trash cans that the wind was now blowing down the street.

Betty approached Edie's table, and they both looked out the window and saw that the wind was also blowing most of the remaining leaves off the trees. It made it easier to see the old house down the street. Betty and Edie smiled

when they noticed several squirrels scattered in the front yard of the old house, as if they were attending a neighborhood party. Betty motioned to a chair and asked if she might have a seat at Edie's table. Edie nodded her head, and her eyes brightened when Betty spoke to her.

Betty motioned to the brown brick house and asked, "Does anyone live in the house with all of those squirrels?" Edie had lived at Happy Visions for several years, and she carried the history of the street like an old story she had read many times before.

Before Edie could reply, the two women watched as an old man walked across the leaf-littered yard to the old, rusty mailbox. He was bent over and wore an old, green army jacket. It looked like a coat that at one time had been part of a uniform. It must not have had buttons, because the old man held it closed tightly with his hands, bracing himself against the cold November wind.

As they watched the man, Betty asked Edie if she knew about the house and the mysterious old man. Edie's face

lit up when she began to speak about the stranger who now stood at the mailbox looking to the cloudy gray sky.

"His name is 'Sarge,'" said Edie. "At least that is what everyone in the neighborhood calls him. He served in the army in World War II and in the Korean War. His lawn used to be the best-kept lawn on the street. He would often stand outside and say hello to people who stopped by to ask for his advice. They wanted to find out how to make their lawns look like his."

Edie continued and said that a few years ago Sarge's wife suddenly passed away. "We are not sure if she was the one who made him mow the lawn, but after she died, he quit mowing it. Now, he lives alone … like a recluse. The neighbors still notice Sarge's lawn—especially since he does not care for it the way he once did. They mow it every now and then to help him out. Sometimes Sarge comes outside to get the mail, but most days he sits in a chair at the front window and watches what is happening on the street. He must not have family, because he never

has visitors … except the mailman."

Betty thanked Edie for this inside information and quickly walked through the brightly lit hallway that led to the back patio. She found Elaine, Adele, and Mildred sitting on the old metal lawn chairs. The cold November wind did not seem to bother them, and the colorful white sparkles that surrounded the women were flying all over the patio. It was beginning to look like someone had put the Christmas lights up a little too early this year!

"What did you find out?" Mildred asked. Betty told them what Edie had shared with her about the old war veteran named "Sarge." When Betty mentioned that he seldom had visitors, the Patio Club began talking about Thanksgiving.

"Can you imagine?" said Elaine. "It's almost Thanksgiving and that guy has no visitors and no family!"

Betty spoke up. "He probably eats TV dinners for Thanksgiving. At least that is what I would do! All that

mess! I used to spend hours cooking, and then everyone ate what I had prepared in about fifteen minutes. Then it was time to get up and start doing dishes. Boy, am I glad I don't have to do the dishes anymore!"

Mildred laughed and said she felt the same way. "In some ways," she said, "you put all that pressure on yourself to make a big meal, and you forget that it is the best holiday of all ... a time to be grateful for what you have."

At that point, Adele suggested they look to the sky to watch a video of the old veteran's life. The women were so grateful for the gift of being able to watch a video in the sky of someone's life. It always gave them information that they needed to help someone. As the women of the Patio Club looked up, a red-tailed hawk floated high overhead. The sky was colored a deep navy and orange from the setting sun. Suddenly, the video of Sarge's life began to play.

First, Sarge appeared as a happy child, standing at a pond with a fishing rod and friends. The video continued

and Sarge was now a serious young man standing at attention and wearing an army uniform. Next, a family photo in a picture frame showed Sarge with a beautiful wife wearing white and one young child. Finally, Sarge was alone on the street in front of the old, brown brick house. The women watched as it all passed by so quickly—just like life.

"That's it!" yelled Mildred. "We have to invite Sarge to Thanksgiving dinner at Happy Visions. But how can we do that?" Smiles crossed the faces of Elaine, Adele, Betty, and Mildred. It was actually Elaine's idea to "go on a trip," as she called it. "Let's make a plan to invite Walter over for Thanksgiving!"

As the women sat on the patio offering their ideas, Walter the dog slowly walked through the door and onto the patio. The women looked at Walter and then looked at each other and smiled as if they all had the same idea.

Mildred winked and said, "Let's have Walter sort of *escape* to the old man's house on Thanksgiving morning,"

she said this knowing that they were the ones who would help Walter finally make it past the fence that the squirrels went under each day.

"Yes," Elaine cheered! "Tonight, after dinner, we can use treats and train Walter to go through the fence and walk down the sidewalk to the old man's house."

They were getting more and more excited. Adele was smiling and said, "Then we can have Walter give the old veteran an invitation to Thanksgiving dinner at Happy Visions!" Just the thought of inviting the old veteran brought joy to all of them.

"I guess we *could* just walk through the old wooden gate and head down the street to Sarge's ourselves," said Betty. "But, if Sarge sees this bunch of women who sparkle coming across his front lawn, *he might think he's died and gone to heaven!*"

The Patio Club laughed at Betty's joke. Then they launched their plan that would take place on Thursday

morning to get the old reclusive veteran named Sarge to join the residents for Thanksgiving dinner. They would have to work quickly to train old Walter the retirement home dog to walk through the back gate and down the street to Sarge's. Then Walter would use his big paw and scratch on the veteran's front door to deliver a special Thanksgiving invitation made by the women.

It turned out that Walter was very easy to train. Late that night, the four women snuck leftover food from dinner and they made a break with Walter through the back gate. They spread leftover pieces of meat from dinner from the back patio all along the tree-lined street and up the sidewalk that led to Sarge's front door. The front door was dark green with chips of paint peeled off from years of neglect. Hanging on the door was an old wreath that had apparently been there for years. The Patio Club noticed that pasted to the front window of the house was an American flag sticker and another shiny sticker that said, "U.S. Army."

After the Patio Club walked Walter back to Happy Visions, they decided to go through their plan one more time to make sure Walter would follow the path of treats that led to Sarge's front door. That was when the Patio Club saw what appeared to be a woman in a bright white gown standing on Sarge's front lawn. The Patio Club was surprised to see her standing there! The women approached her, and it seemed as though they could see right through her!

The woman in the sparkling white gown was very excited to see the Patio Club. "Thank you", she said happily with a smile on her face. "You are the answer to my prayer!" she said, "Sarge's real name is Richard, but everyone actually calls him 'Sarge.'"

The woman in white continued saying, "Sarge doesn't do anything special for Thanksgiving except sit and eat another TV dinner. I am so happy to see that you are training this kindhearted dog to invite Sarge to Thanksgiving dinner at Happy Visions!"

Elaine, Adele, Betty, and Mildred were *stunned* by the woman in the white sparkling gown standing on the lawn. *"Who is she?"* Adele whispered to the others. That's when the woman introduced herself.

"My name is Mercy. I am Sarge's wife. I died a few years ago. Sarge is *so* stubborn that he still lives alone and won't let anyone help him. Our son, Harvey, passed away last year. Since then, Sarge has not been outside of that house except to talk to the mailman and go buy those darn TV dinners!" After Mercy spoke, she stood staring in wonder at the brilliant orange sparkles that swirled around the happy group of women and their dog.

Mildred spoke for the group and said to Mercy, "We call ourselves the Patio Club because we sit outside on the patio each day at Happy Visions Retirement home. It's just up the street. We are delighted that we are being called to help Sarge"

"Don't worry," Betty told Mercy. "We will take care of your wish and prayers for Sarge. We will invite him to eat

Thanksgiving dinner tomorrow at Happy Visions." Upon hearing this, Mercy laughed and thanked them. The she clapped her hands and was gone just as quickly as she had appeared.

The women of the Patio Club walked Walter back to Happy Visions. They were excited about their plan that would take place the next day. As they walked through the back gate, they were still talking about Mercy, the woman in white who they'd met standing on Sarge's lawn.

The following morning, Thanksgiving announced itself with the smell of pumpkin pies baking, as the staff prepared for the special meal for that holiday. Adele went into the dining room when the staff was not looking and set a place setting for Sarge at Edie's table. The women decided to seat Sarge right next to Edie. The women of the club knew that Edie would have the most current information about the neighborhood to share with Sarge. The Patio Club kept it a secret and told no one. They wanted Sarge to be the surprise special guest for Thanksgiving dinner at Happy Visions.

The Patio Club went into the craft room and used markers and colored paper to make a Thanksgiving card for Sarge. Walter would deliver the card to Sarge at his front door. The card read,

Oh Mercy! Not another TV dinner!

Please follow Walter the dog to Happy Visions Retirement Home for Thanksgiving dinner. We have saved a special seat just for you.

Love,

The Patio Club

Thanksgiving dinner was scheduled for noon, and residents and guests began making their way to the dining room at eleven o'clock. The women of the Patio Club walked Walter to the back gate and silently unlocked and opened it. Walter quickly began following and eating the training treats that still littered the leaf-covered sidewalk.

The old dog did his part and slowly walked up to Sarge's front door. He began scratching on the door and barking. Slowly, the green door with peeling paint began to open. The old man dressed in a green army jacket stood there. He said, "Well, will you look here! Hey big fellow!"

Walter dropped the colorful Thanksgiving invitation that the women had made, and it landed at Sarge's feet. Slowly, Sarge bent to pick it up and began reading it out loud as Walter tilted his head like he understood the words. Sarge laughed as he read:

~

Oh Mercy! Not another TV dinner!

Please follow Walter the dog to Happy Visions Retirement home for Thanksgiving dinner. We have saved a special seat just for you.

Love,

The Patio Club

Sarge laughed and said to Walter, "That darn Mercy! She said she would come back to haunt me if I didn't go out for Thanksgiving dinner. I guess she meant it! Let's go, big fellow!"

Sarge closed his front door, and the old man and the dog walked up the street to Happy Visions Retirement Home. The leaves made a swishing sound as they walked, and a faint trail of red sparkles followed behind the old veteran and the dog that now escorted him.

Outside the front door of Happy Visions, the sparkling women of the Patio Club welcomed Sarge. Edie stood in the hallway that led to the dining room. When she saw Sarge, she held out her arm so she could escort him to her table. Sarge was wearing his old army coat, and it seemed to announce to everyone that a very special visitor was joining them for Thanksgiving dinner.

As they all gave thanks to God for the many blessings

of each day, Sarge bowed his head and silently thanked Mercy for looking after him like she said she would—especially on Thanksgiving.

After dinner, Elaine, Adele, Betty and Mildred walked outside and closed the gate where Walter had made a break for Sarge's house. The four women looked to the sky one last time to watch Sarge's story as it continued to unfold. In the video, Sarge was sitting at the table in the dining room of Happy Visions Retirement Home. A big smile was on his face. Sitting next to him was a beautiful woman dressed in white who no one could see. It was Mercy, and she was smiling. Sarge seemed to sense she was there and he was filled with the kind of gratitude that comes easily at Thanksgiving.

≈

Thanksgiving is a good time to thank all of the angels, both here and beyond, who look after us each day. It is a good time to express gratitude for the small surprises that have the ability to touch our hearts, no matter what

age we are—especially at Thanksgiving time.

Happy Thanksgiving from the Patio Club!

The End.

The Patio Clubs Story

IN NOVEMBER OF 2016, I began writing fictional stories for retirement and assisted living communities. This occurred because of a simple request from an older gentleman in his 80s who asked if I could write a story about people "their age." Writing and telling stories has always come easily to me. I happily said , "yes." I was excited at the challenge and have written a story each month since then. They are about a fictional retirement/ assisted living community named *Happy Visions*. Each month I read to retirement and assisted living communities. The joy of doing this is overwhelming.

In July of 2017, I was reading to a group of older women as they sat outside *on the patio* in the shade. The women's ages reached up to 95. When I left the patio that day, I decided at that moment to write a story for them called "The Patio Club." The series began with that story.

The stories I write come effortlessly to me. It is as if I am divinely inspired. As I began writing the first story in the Patio Club series, I was so surprised as I watched the story come to life. It is the story of two sets of sisters, Elaine and Adele from New Jersey, and Mildred and Betty from Kentucky. They made a pact that when they died they would meet up and visit retirement and assisted living communities.

Imagine my surprise—because in real life Elaine and Adele (sisters) were my aunts from New Jersey, and Betty (my mother) and Mildred (my aunt) were sisters from Kentucky! My Aunt Mildred was the last one to join The Patio Club. She passed away earlier in 2017. The Patio Club™ stories now touch people from around the country and hopefully someday from around the world.

My dream is that The Patio Club™ series will be read to the people in assisted living, memory and Hospice care communities. As I read each month to these special people, I realized that it is often difficult to visit loved ones who are in the assisted living population. What I have found is that reading a story seems to transform everyone from the reader to the listener. I have seen people with all kinds of health challenges perk up when listening to the joyful adventures of The Patio Club™. They are in the present moment as they listen and during that time there is nothing wrong with them.

My wish is that people will take the adventure of reading a story (about 12 to 15 minutes) from The Patio Club Series to a loved one. It will transform the visit from one where it may be difficult to find something to talk about, to one where both the reader and listener are moved beyond words.

With gratitude and love,

- Caryn

Acknowledgments

THE PATIO CLUB is dedicated to my aunts Elaine, Adele, Mildred, and my mother Betty. Although the characters in the Patio Club are fictional, they are based on these important women who impacted my life.

Special thanks to my sons Carson and Cooper, as well as, family and friends who have listened to these stories. They have enthusiastically cheered for me to follow my dream to write and illustrate stories that bring joy and adventure to the lives of others.

Finally, I am grateful to God for the gifts He has given me to serve the people in assisted living, memory and Hospice care.

About the Author

CARYN BEGAN WRITING children's stories for her children in the 1990s. In 2016, as she read children's stories to assisted living communities, residents asked her to write a story "for people their age." That was how the adventure of writing for the adult and assisted population began.

Since that time, Caryn has written a monthly series called The Patio Club™. It takes place at a retirement home/assisted living community named Happy Visions. The Patio Club™ are the first stories published by Caryn for that age group. The stories have captured the attention of people of all ages across the country.

The Patio Club™ stories are a bridge between the reader and the listener. Family and friends that visit assisted living, memory and Hospice care communities may struggle for something to talk about. Reading a story like The Patio Club™ to these special residents takes them on an adventure without them ever having to leave the room. It creates an opening for some interesting conversations!

Caryn lives in Colorado. She has two grown sons, Carson and Cooper

www.ingramcontent.com/pod-product-compliance
Lightning Source LLC
Chambersburg PA
CBHW041221040426

42443CB00002B/44